Proverbs *of* Success

The Heart & Soul of Highly Effective People

JOHN GROGAN

Evergreen
PRESS

Proverbs of Success
by John Grogan

ISBN 1-58169-045-2
For Worldwide Distribution
Printed in Canada

Evergreen Press
An Imprint of Genesis Communications, Inc.
P.O. Box 91011 • Mobile, AL 36691
800-367-8203
Email: GenesisCom@aol.com

TABLE OF CONTENTS

DEDICATION

This book is dedicated to some very special people who love me in spite of my frailties and infinite disposition to reveal my clay feet:

My daughters Kristina and Kathy;

Their mother who has proved faithful as a single parent;

My wife Jackie who is a living testimony to loyalty, decency, and irrefutable proof that God is the author of second chances;

My twin brother Thomas—a prince among men—whose wisdom and pursuit of character has been incalculable in guiding this pilgrim;

The many whom I have encountered along the way—those who blessed and those who afflicted according to my needs.

INTRODUCTION

Proverbs of Success has been 30 years in the making. It's a book of wisdom born of pain—very often, unnecessary pain—which, nevertheless, brought about needed changes in my life and in my business.

There are three main reasons why we decide to make changes in our lives. We can change because we get excited about the prospects the new behavior will bring—unfortunately, this appeals to the emotions and is usually short lived. We can change as a result of knowledge, new insights, or additional information—this is an appeal to the intellect and more often results in permanent improvement. Or, we can change because our present actions result in so much discomfort that we are left with no options—we are driven to take action. This book is an attempt to help you avoid the last situation.

Proverbs of Success is not a book of quick fixes or false promises. However, it will give you principles that will help you steer your course in the way you truly desire to go. It is a book, above all, for those who seek to shorten the timeline to greater peace, self-acceptance, and worthwhile productivity.

LEADERSHIP

Leadership is not in the title; it's in the execution. Effective leaders enable others to do what they're doing.

A leader's greatness is determined by the quality of his or her advisors.

Many times we tend to overstudy a situation. It's ready, aim, aim, aim, fire, when it should be ready, fire, aim (that's correct). Ready, aim, fire is legitimate when the cost to change the outcome is high. When the cost to change the outcome is low, get into action quickly.

We have to learn when to take action. As with our health, it often isn't surgery that kills, but delayed surgery.

The number one complaint of people in the workplace: The only time I ever see my manager/boss/supervisor is when I make a mistake. The number one complaint among middle management...is the same thing.

You can always tell how well you're doing by the number of detractors you have. Jealousy is a light sleeper and is easily aroused.

As a leader, whether pastor, parent, or manager, never be scandalized by anything someone confides in you. If they perceive an arched eyebrow or a gasp of surprise, they will regard it as a judgment. Your first response should be, "That's interesting."

One of the greatest pieces of advice I ever received regarding a coaching style of leadership versus an autocratic style of leadership: People accept what they help create.

As a leader, approximately 25% of your people will *like* you for the *wrong* reasons. Approximately 25% of your people will *like* you for the *right* reasons. Approximately 25% of your people will *dislike* you for the *wrong* reasons. And approximately 25% of your people will *dislike* you for the *right* reasons. It's only the last 25% that you should be concerned about.

In many cases, committees are made up of people who individually can do nothing and together decide that nothing can be done.

Open door policy versus a screen door policy: An open door policy conveys the message that the group has unrestricted access to the leader. This can result in never-ending interruptions for the leader as members of the group rely more and more on the leader to do all the thinking. A screen door policy sets forth specific times for caucusing, thus enabling the leader to more than scratch the surface regarding their own "to do" list, while at the same time eliminating the need to hide behind a closed door.

One of the major things leaders can do for their people is to encourage them through positive affirmation because most people tend to magnify their weaknesses and gloss over their strengths.

One plus God equals a majority.

The wise leader works hard at unity. Meaningful achievement is brought about through corporiety. Individuality is all elbows; it separates and isolates. Unity is lost and the power to accomplish is dissipated.

We have to move from maintenance to mission.

A saying that came out of the 16th century is still applicable today: "It is impossible to be a hero to your own valet for your valet sees you stripped of all braid and brocade." It is most difficult to be a hero to those who know you best. If you can be a hero to your spouse and children, you're quite a person.

Wise leaders surround themselves with the best possible advisors. These advisors have perfected their particular skills. They are mentally tough and resolute. They are physically in shape—they have staying power. And they are dedicated to serving, aiding, and supporting the leader. Weak leaders are readily threatened by able subordinates, but strong leaders surround themselves with such people and are not intimidated by the giftedness of their followers.

Emerson once said, "Great men of all time are lovers of their kind." Faith in people and regard for people are unfailing marks of true greatness.

$100
$50

MONEY

Most companies, it seems, "pay to the position" rather than to the performance. Instead, you should reward results rather than mere activity.

If we are willing to do more than we are paid to do, eventually we will be paid for more than we do.

It would be a quantum leap for many in the service industry to realize that they represent the overhead and the customer represents the profit.

Don't buy on the "come"; don't spend money before it's in hand. Restraint and self-discipline is better than a warrior who takes a city.

The old 80/20 rule still pretty much applies. Eighty percent of your business will come from twenty percent of your customers or clients. Twenty percent of your staff will bring you eighty percent of your problems. Eighty percent of your results will come from twenty percent of the things you do. Pursue the vital few rather than the trivial many.

The person who always keeps score will never appreciate what the giving person has discovered: You very well may reap from a field different than the one in which you sowed.

The more we own, the more we can become owned by what we possess because the more we'll have to maintain.

Don't strive to become rich, rather strive to become a person of character.

This is a law of the universe: If you help others to prosper, you yourself must prosper.

If I give you a dollar and you give me a dollar, we both still have just a dollar. But if I give you an idea and you give me an idea, we will be dollars ahead.

Great societies are not measured by the amount of wealth they accumulate, but by how they treat their poor.

Never hesitate to spend money to create memories.

The perplexity of a horse show: People investing $25,000 in a horse so they can win a $15 ribbon.

"When you start wearing silk pajamas, it's very difficult to get up early in the morning for prayer." *(Eddie Arcaro)*

If you are in sales and/or marketing, the first thing people will notice about you is your tie and your shoes. Never hesitate to invest wisely in both.

The problem is not the high cost of living, the problem is the cost of living high.

We move towards what we think about. This is the reason we can never become successful if we focus on our debt or our weaknesses.

Don't be greedy. It is better to have 10 percent of a cow than to have 90 percent of a chicken.

Two of the modern conveniences that have the potential for great harm are the ATM machine and the aptly named "swipe" machine used by grocery stores. With ATM machines, people have a tendency not to keep track of their money as evidenced by the blanket of receipts covering the ground nearby. Money can be too accessible using a credit card in a swipe machine. The temptation to overspend is almost irresistible because there's no exchange of cash. In a week, the steak has been consumed and the consumer is left owing 18% interest on something they no longer have. Three weeks of this and the shopper is buried in debt. At 18% interest, making a minimum payment on the account, it could take the shopper years to pay for that steak!

Everybody wants your money. Their attitude is: "You've got *our* money in your pocket. Our objective is to get *our* money out of *your* pocket and into *our* bank account."

We have to learn to distinguish between needs and wants. Two thirds of us never pay off our credit cards!

Perseverance

Few things will take the place of persistence. It is for want of sustained application that most people fall short of success.

There can be a downside to industriousness. Busyness can keep us running at such hyper fast speed that we never quiet our compulsions and our thoughts in order to bring meaning to our lives.

Facing an opportunity without being ready is a little like preparing your shells at the battle lines. By the time you're ready to shoot, you've been wiped out.

Doing something exactly right is made up of a series of "approximate" rights.

Many people mistake activity for achievement. Motion does not always mean progress.

We all relish mountaintop experiences with God, but fruit trees do not grow on mountain tops. God wants us down in the valleys producing, tending, and harvesting fruit.

Perseverance, not perfection, is the key to winning at life.

Weariness can cause us to become impatient; on impulse, we take an action...perhaps a wrong action.

We're either fishing or merely maintaining an aquarium.

"By perseverance," Spurgeon said, "the snail reached the Ark."

At the Olympic games in Mexico City in 1968, Steven Acquairy, marathon runner from Tanzania, finished two hours behind the second to last runner. When asked by a reporter why he even bothered to finish, he replied, "My country didn't send me 9000 miles to start a race—they sent me 9000 miles to finish a race."

The accomplishments of tomorrow are established by the habits developed today.

Contrary to widely held belief, we are not made in the test, but rather we are revealed by the test. We are made from day to day.

Endurance: Taken from two Greek words—up and hold. It's a military term carrying the idea of abiding, bearing with, not fainting or suffering the loss of courage. Endurance describes the quality of carrying on under problematic circumstances without passive resignation, to persist with hope and fortitude while actively resisting both weariness and a surrender to fear and doubt.

Doing little things makes big things happen.

Service

Some companies are downplaying customer service, contending that it is irrelevant in lieu of price. This is an opportunity for the "Davids" out there in the marketplace to overcome the giants and create their niche.

> The 3/11 rule: People who are satisfied or happy with your service will, on the average, tell three people. People who are dissatisfied will, on the average, tell eleven people.

There are four levels of service: 1) Hide and seek. You can't find someone when you need service because they're avoiding you. 2) Surrender. You've got them trapped in the open, there are zero options, and so they agree to wait on you. 3) Voluntary. They exercise a healthy approach to seeking you out to see if they can help you. 4) Assumptive. They anticipate your needs, and their help is given before you have to ask.

It's five times easier to lose a customer over poor service than over poor products.

People don't buy light bulbs; they buy the light they get from light bulbs. People buy *benefits;* they don't buy *products*.

Be careful about using industry jargon your customers or clients might be confused by or not understand. I once heard a bank employee tell a call-in customer that the teller they wanted to speak with was "out of her cage."

It is five times more difficult to win a new customer than it is to retain an existing one. I've seen more small businesses close their doors as a result of failing to grasp this consideration.

A great story is told about the late Bishop Fulton J. Sheen. When he sat down in a restaurant at a hotel, a waitress (who obviously had a job and not a mission) asked in a most perfunctory way what he wanted to order.

"Two eggs over easy...and a kind word," the good bishop requested. Before long, the waitress returned with his order. She placed the meal before him with a show of indifference, turned on her heels, and began to walk away. Bishop Sheen called out after her, asking about the kind word. Without missing a step, she growled over her shoulder, "Don't eat them eggs!"

We can sometimes learn valuable things from difficult people.

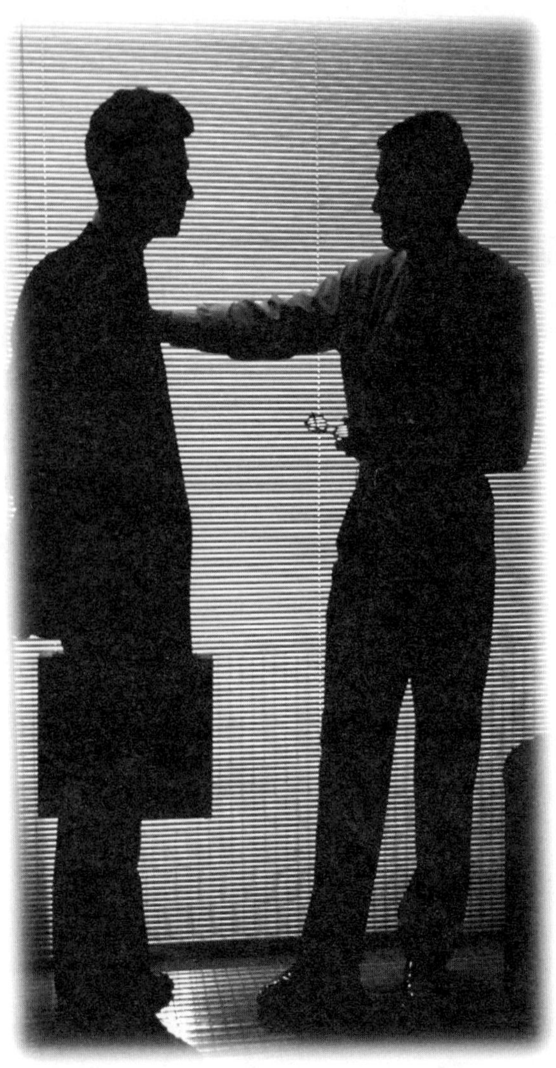

Compassion

Be brutal about time, but gentle with people.

Kindness, the Talmud says, is the highest wisdom.

How to take the sting out of having to ask a personal question: Ask permission to do so. Most people will be so curious as to what the question might be, they will not refuse.

A seven step formula to giving correction that will accomplish the job without alienating the other party or wounding their spirit:

1. Ensure as much as possible that you have the right person.
2. Correct in private. Reducing a person to pulp in front of their peers only gives birth to resentment.
3. Preface with a kind word.
4. Criticize the act and not the person.
5. Tell or show the person how it should have been handled.
6. Ask for their cooperation so that it won't

be repeated in the future. It is important that you have eye contact when asking this question. Make sure they agree with your proposal, even if it's only with a head nod.

7. Part on a friendly note.

"Pre-calling" eliminates surprises. Tell people, when you can, what's going to take place in the future. Most people don't handle surprises very well.

Separate the person from the problem. Don't ask, "Why did you do it?"; instead, ask "What caused you to do it that way?" *Why* is asking for reasons and causes the person to become defensive. *What* uncovers causes and is less threatening.

Winners in a confrontation don't really win, and losers never forget

We are a people who have thin skins and thick hearts. We are so quick to take offense. God wants us to have thicker skins and softer, more tender compassionate hearts.

Judgment tempered by mercy is truth that sets free.

We are a society today that elevates to hero status those who put others down. To trump someone at their expense is really a hollow victory.

God is not our Comforter in order to make us comfortable. God is our Comforter so that we may bring comfort to others.

Discouragement

Failure is not permanent; it is experimentation. Henry Ford overlooked putting a reverse gear in his original model, but it wasn't fatal. Giving up, like suicide, is a permanent solution to a temporary problem.

Most people get little out of life because they don't expect very much.

The real tragedy of giving up is to be able to see how close we came to success and know that, had we renewed our hope one more time, we might have broken through to success.

People with low self-esteem usually base their self-image on who they know, what they own, or what they can do.

Suicide is the severest form of self-criticism.

Some people are born crying, live complaining, and will die disappointed.

Low self value—low expectations. Low expectations—low yield.

Man's own folly ruins his life, yet he shakes his fist at God.

The reason God can't use many of us is because we keep crawling off the altar of self-sacrifice.

Military surrender is forced; spiritual surrender is voluntary.

If there is not hope for the future, there is no strength for the present.

Failure is temporary; quitting is forever.

There's a story told about a prizefighter being interviewed by a reporter who asks, "What kind of fighter are you?"

The fighter quickly answered, "I'm always up or getting up."

When he was falling to the mat, in his mind he was getting up. This is what we have to do when we're knocked down by circumstances in life.

We are tempted to give up when we make our conclusions in the middle of the matter.

Employees

It's easier to "hire attitude" and "train skill" than to "hire skill" and try to change attitude. You can pay a person with a bad attitude three times as much money, and all you have is a person with a bad attitude who's three times richer.

Man must be taught as if you taught him not; and things new proposed as merely things forgot.

Correct a fool and they will despise you. Correct a wise person and they will be wiser still.

Many leaders are too insecure to trust or to empower their people. They never seem able to grasp the wisdom of the old Chinese proverb: When you collect the power, you disperse the people. When you disperse the power, you gather the people.

The conventional definition of *management leadership* espoused by some high profile business gurus is: Management is getting the job done through others. However, this can easily become manipulation because the emphasis is placed on "getting the job done." If we place the emphasis on *people* rather than on *objectives*, a better definition of management leadership might be: management is getting the job done by helping people to be all that they can be on the job.

The critic,
the complainer,
the malcontent, are
expendable when a
company must
restructure.

We must be exhortative with our people rather than merely motivational. Motivation appeals to the emotions, and people don't make long-term behavioral changes because of their emotions. Exhortation appeals to a person's will, and it is in the will where people change.

You will get better work from an untrained, willing apprentice than from a skilled rebel.

There are basically three reasons a person does not perform a task:

1. *Doesn't know how* to do the task. This is a training problem.
2. *Can't* do it. This could be a problem dealing with aptitude.
3. *Won't* do it. This could be due to an excessive, acceptable rate of productivity, or it could indicate an attitudinal problem.

Some people are trapped in the old and blind to the new. The story is told about a business consultant who observed a staff member for several days taking a large stack of computer printout forms into an executive's office, but nothing ever seemed to be done with them. When the consultant inquired as to who's office it was, he was told that it was the office of one of the vice-presidents...and that he had died six months earlier—an example of ritual over function.

Commitment empowers us to persevere. The pro knows that the resistance is always in direct proportion to the prize.

S.W.S.W.S.W.G.O. (Some will; some won't; so what; go on.) Destiny hates a laggard.

Opportunity is sometimes spelled RISK... and risk is sometimes spelled FOOLISH. Sometimes we've got to be willing to risk looking foolish in the eyes of others.

In 1960, the Democratic party of San Antonio held a fundraiser at the Alamo. The guest speaker of the evening was the front runner, Senator John Kennedy. Three quarters of the way through the evening, Kennedy leaned over and asked the mayor if there was a back way out, that he had to get to Houston for an early morning breakfast with some influential business leaders. The mayor looked at Kennedy and said indignantly, "Senator, if there was a back way out, there wouldn't have been an Alamo!" Sometime in our life we have to cut off all our exits, draw a line in the sand, and say, "Here is where I make my stand. I retreat no further because of my fears and doubts."

"Our doubts are traitors," Shakespeare said, "and make us lose the good we oft might win by fearing to attempt."

When high performance people are forced to retreat, they think of it as simply attacking in a different direction.

The Tongue

The thing that makes the grapevine so menacing is that as the gossip travels along, it only gets worse, it never gets better.

The rule for "bucket dumping" (passing along problems): Always *dump up*—one of the responsibilities of a manager, leader, or supervisor is to receive the contents of our bucket. If we *dump laterally* (on our peers) we contribute to the problem. If we *dump down* on the people we supervise, we place a load on them they are not prepared or equipped to handle.

The one thing we cannot conceal is our vocabulary. When we speak, our minds are on parade.

Words are like fire and can burn to destruction, and we can't reverse the damage they can do.

Every action of our life reflects what we fill our life with. If we fill our life with sports, we speak sports. If we fill it with news, we speak news. We cannot give away what we do not have.

Words are containers. These containers hold either life or death for those who hear them.

Beware of flattering lips or a boastful tongue—where they are, deception is close at hand.

The tongue has the power of life and death. We can rip, shred, belittle, or pierce like a bayonet with our tongue; or we can edify, encourage, lift up, and exhort with it.

Brevity is power. Some people speak when they feel a need to say something; others speak when they have something to say.

To be successful in selling, you've got to let people know three things: 1) who you are; 2) what you do; and 3) where you do it. The more widely you broadcast this information in the shortest possible time frame will determine the velocity of your lift off and the height of your initial success.

People are more convinced by the intensity of your beliefs than by the soundness of your reasoning.

Watch how you talk to yourself. We spend 80-85% of our time "talking" to ourselves. We think a lot and we are usually at center stage of our thoughts. Here's the key question: If you had a friend who talked to you the way you talk to yourself, would you hang around them?

RELATIONSHIPS

All human relations are based on needs being met. Human need is the point of contact. The cooperative stage is where the attitude is one of mutual collaboration. Unfortunately, many times because of pride or greed, one of the parties wants to dominate the other. This causes the one being dominated to retaliate which, in turn, results in increased pressure by the one who is in charge. At this point, the dominated one usually moves from retaliation to isolation.

One of the great keys to building strong relational bridges with people is the willingness to waste time with them.

The highest form of manipulation is withdrawal—either physical, mental, or emotional—because there's nothing the other person can do about it.

The word *confrontation* conveys a negative image. In truth, confrontation is neutral; it's how it's handled that makes it positive or negative. The whole point of confrontation is to settle the issue and get back to productivity.

We are quickly moving towards becoming a nation of strangers with more home based businesses and more shopping via the Internet. It's growing more difficult to reach people by telephone. Many times when you call someone, you're automatically put through to their voice mail. This will lead to greater isolation and a sense of aloneness.

Truly loving another always involves the surrender of power.

The five progressive steps to a trusting relationship: 1) performance, 2) stating facts, 3) stating opinions, 4) expressing feelings, and 5) truth. The objective is to get to level five as quickly as possible because only in truth is there light, and only in light is there life.

The pathway to a broken relationship: 1) A hurt or wound → 2) Anger → 3) Resentment → 4) Bitterness → 5) Apathy.

One of the most important things we can do in effectively communicating with others is to maintain eye contact with the other person when they're speaking. We will excuse the speaker if their eyes wander a bit as they are composing their speech, but if the listener lets their eyes wander, it says to the speaker, "I'm discounting the importance of your message," or worse, "You don't count."

The easiest thing to give away in a relationship is one's body; the most difficult is one's heart.

Sometimes learned behavior has to be unlearned when a person transitions into a different cultural climate. To establish eye contact with a stranger in some societal environments is tantamount to throwing down the gauntlet. In business dealings, avoidance of eye contact usually is interpreted as guile.

With real-time information, you have to trust each other.

A good relationship complements; a poor relationship competes.

If we agreed on everything, one of us wouldn't be necessary. That's why they make vanilla and chocolate.

When we lie down for the last time, the thing that will occupy our minds the most will not be anything material, it will be relationships.

A father's love keeps sowing, does not keep score, and does it for the glory of God and not the recognition of his family. One day he will reap a wonderful and abundant harvest.

You either love people and use things, or you love things and use people.

At the very bottom of hell, according to Dante (the author of the classical works *The Divine Comedy* and *The Inferno*), are three arch traitors—Cassius and Brutus, friends of Caesar who killed him, and Judas Iscariot. They are resigned to the worst of hell's punishments not so much because they killed their masters but rather because they betrayed the trust extended to them by their masters. It is fraud that eventually robs people of their ability to trust, resulting in the severing of relationships.

LEARNING

Experience is a good teacher, but it is a tardy one. We should learn the lessons before having to go through the experience.

Around the age of 33, calcification begins to set in. The result can be "hardening of the categories" where we think everyone else is out of step except us.

Those who wholeheartedly ascribe to the philosophy "If it ain't broke, don't fix it," will be eclipsed by those who are always fine-tuning the model.

A consultant is someone who takes your watch and tells you what time it is.

An efficiency expert is someone who shows you the best way to do a job. An effectiveness expert is someone who can show you the best job to do.

We cannot function on what we don't know; school is never out for the pro.

One definition of knowledge vs wisdom: Knowledge is when we learn from our own mistakes. Wisdom is when we learn from someone else's mistakes.

One reason for wisdom born of pain: Too soon old; too late smart.

We cannot function on what we do not know. Read the Bible to be wise; believe it to be safe; practice it to be virtuous.

Learning, according to Mike Vance, usually progresses through four stages of growth: 1) *The Unconscious Incompetent*—they don't know that they don't know. 2) *The Conscious Incompetent*—They know that they don't know. 3) *The Conscious Competent*—they know but they have to think about it before they do it. 4) *The Unconscious Competent*—they do it automatically without having to think it through.

The great lessons of life are learned in adversity.

Life is a continual process of learning and discovering things new. From time to time, we encounter ideas, facts, or situations which are inconsistent with our cherished beliefs or perception of reality. When this happens, we either change our beliefs or defend them by rejecting the new information. The decision to be openminded has to be made again and again.

NW
NNW
WNW
W
WSW
SW
SSW
S
SSE
SE
ESE
E
ENE
NE
NNE

Goals

If we don't have a goal to get us to a predetermined target, we begin to mistake activity for achievement. We start to shrink our dreams to match our income rather than expand our income to capture our dreams.

God is chairman of the results committee.

Goals develop *knowledge* which answers the question WHAT. What are we after?

Planning/strategizing develops *understanding* which answers the question HOW. "How exactly are we going to do this?"

Prioritizing develops *timing* which answers the question WHEN. When will we execute the various steps?

Purpose develops *wisdom* which answers the question WHY. Why are we doing it this way? Why are we doing this at all?

Goals generate commitment. Our identity comes out of what we are committed to.

Our outlook on life should not be determined by circumstances, but by focus.

Seven out of ten people wind up financially, emotionally, morally, or spiritually broke by age 65.

Fear keeps our dreams at a distance.

It is not wise to advance our blueprints under God's nose. He is not in the business of stamping an approval on our plans.

God doesn't pull us out of deep water to let us drown. He has a plan for us.

If we look back reflectively over our life, we will see that most of the major course changes in our life were not planned. More than ever, we need a good pilot in our life.

God determines what we *may* become. We decide what we *shall* become.

Choices, not chance, determine our destiny.

Failure to set goals leads to an evasion of accountability. To the extent we turn away from accountability, we forsake our vigilance. Without vigilance we float. The insidious thing about floating is that we can become used to it. Floating is a slow motion pretense of being busy. It's like treading water—you never get anywhere.

Reaching our objective without a planned strategy is tantamount to laying all the parts of an airliner out on the ground and waiting for it to come together all by itself.

One can quite easily determine one's destiny by asking a two-word question: *What then?* For example: "I want to graduate from school." *What then?* "Get a good job." *What then?* "Get married, raise a family." *What then?* "Enjoy a nice retirement." *What then?* "Well…die, I suppose." *What then?*

TIME

When asked what contributed to his success as supreme allied commander during WWII, Eisenhower said that one of the things he found helpful to remember was that the urgent things were seldom important, and the important things were seldom urgent.

Plan for the next day...set priorities.

Vary your work tempo. Remember, even a cheetah doesn't run flat out all day.

Set deadlines not only for tasks, but for activities within a task. Don't spend 30 minutes doing a 15 minute job.

Place the most frequently used items near you. And try to keep both hands free for secondary productive work.

Delegate if possible. Learn a task, pass it on,

and learn a new task. This increases your value. If you voluntarily continue to do a task once you've mastered it, you major in minors and become a high-priced secretary.

Review progress during the day and reprioritize if necessary.

Practice "calculated neglect," especially if you're a perfectionist. Nit-pickers drive others crazy.

Identify your best energy cycle(s) and do your most difficult or mentally challenging tasks during these times. It's tough to work on critical, goal-related, must-be-done today things when your energy level is heading south.

Make use of all the latest time saving technological gadgetry and don't be afraid of it. It may take a little time to learn, but it will be well worth it in the long run.

Try to innovate your routines for maximum efficiency; e.g., think of time in terms of "segments"—15 minutes to a segment. How many segments will I use for lunch? How many will I invest in idle chit-chat with my peers who aren't going to conduct any business with me? Conversely, if I'm "going to school," I might invest several time segments with them.

Don't let others' emergencies become your urgencies. Highly productive people assert their right to control their schedules.

Brevity is power. When sharing your thoughts or ideas, especially with busy people, think it through and then give them the "elevator version." This is a term that came out of the Pentagon and means, "Tell me as much as you could if we rode up an elevator from one floor to the next." In other words, keep it short and let them ask questions.

Cluster your outgoing telephone calls if practical, but more importantly, group your return phone calls. Prioritize them using three categories: Good-shot...better-shot...best-shot. Those receiving my *good-shot* get a return call at my convenience. Those receiving my *better-shot* receive a call back today. Those receiving my *best-shot* receive a a call as soon as I can break free from what is occupying me at the moment.

Implement a "time out" or "quiet time" to reenergize or refocus on priorities.

In many cases it's not a matter of too much to do, or too little time in which to do it, it's a matter of priorities. Some "monkeys" (responsibilities) we are obliged to carry. Stop volunteering to carry other people's monkeys

One of the most insidious cheaters of productivity is a common game many people play—the Scenario Game. We sit around nursing that third cup of coffee, rehashing some thoughts or plans we've been over a hundred times: "If I/we do this, that will probably happen; if we do that, this will probably happen." Forever planning, never implementing.

To save time, conduct informal meetings standing up. This conveys a clear message to your visitor that time is precious and this meeting will be short. If they insist on being seated, you might consider Admiral Hyman Rickover's method for ending overlong visits—he simply cut two inches off the front legs of the chair in front of his desk.

The time/value ratio: Is what I'm doing now worth the time it's taking me to do it? If the answer is no, I should stop doing it and do something else. This should be a thought that reoccurs all day long like a chorus in a song.

8

Problems

There are three choices or options open to us regarding a problem at work: 1) We can continue to work to try and change it. 2) We can accept it as part of the status quo. 3) Or we can leave the job if the cost of acceptance is too high. When we fully appreciate this, it voids our license to grouse.

A complaint has two dimensions: 1) content and 2) feelings. Focus on the feelings, and things get worse.

Winners don't keep score, but they do document, especially when storm clouds are gathering and a confrontation is a growing possibility.

The word *crisis* in Chinese means opportunity.

A formula for solving problems: State the problem, preferably in writing. Writing causes us to think in concrete, specific terms rather than in general, abstract terms. Second, analyze the issues involved. Third, define your strategy or goal. Fourth, come up with tactics, that is, plans on how to accomplish it.

A wise aphorism says that it is to a person's honor to avoid strife...but fools are quick to quarrel.

The five ways we can handle conflict:

1. Intimidation
2. Irritation
3. Suppression
4. Avoidance
5. Resolution

It's better to know God than to have answers.

Worry is pagan. Worry says God's arm is too short.

Lessons from God of great significance almost never happen in shallow water. If we are in water that is only ankle deep, we can scurry back up onto the shore. We do not scurry out of neck high water, but rather have to work our way through it.

God has never bought into the idea that the end justifies the means.

Today, cooperation is not just a social pleasantry, it's an economic necessity. Reciprocity comes quickly in the give-and-take world in which we live. We *have to* work together, not merely along side of one another.

Integrity

Fear of man or overzealousness in trying to curry the favor of a rich or influential person can cause one to forsake their integrity.

Clever people can always justify their inconsistencies.

Most people do what is *inspected* rather than what is *expected*.

A fanatic is someone who's more committed to something than we are.

Integrity is often at odds with expediency.

If one is free from the fear of man, then one is free from feeling the need to lie.

"Cosmetic Christianity"—trying to be good on the outside. It will wear you out.

Any church afraid or unwilling to call its people into accountability is basically running a hospital.

We tend to evaluate and criticize others based on their greatest inadequacies. We evaluate ourselves based on our most noble intentions.

If we cannot obey laws and authority we can see, we will never be able to obey an authority we cannot see.

Integrity says "I will not tread on you." It also says, "I will not let you tread on me."

One aspect of integrity towards self is

checking up on ourselves. I'm reminded of the little boy making a phone call from the neighborhood drugstore. He asks the person on the other end of the line if he would like to have his lawn mowed. The person says he already has someone who cuts his lawn. After several more attempts to win the prospect over, he says thank you and hangs up the phone. The drugstore owner has overheard the conversation, and wishing to encourage the young lad, exhorts him to hang in there and not grow discouraged.

"Oh, Mr. Martin," the budding young tycoon says, "You don't understand. The person I just called is already a customer of mine, I'm just checking up on myself." Call your office periodically, or have your spouse or a friend call in as a prospect. You may be quite surprised to find out the kind of treatment your customers or prospective clients are receiving.

Growth

They tell the story of Randolph Hearst, publisher and editor of the *San Francisco Examiner*, sending an aide on a worldwide search for a certain painting that he strongly desired for his collection. After an exhaustive search, the aide found the painting—it was already a part of the Hearst collection. Most of us already possess the seeds of greatness within us to reach our genetic promise.

Four important areas for development:

1. Product knowledge
2. Skills for performance
3. Attitude
4. Good habits

Never let today's failures corrupt your new beginnings.

When you fall down, don't stay down. Get up, pull up your socks, and continue the race.

Backsliding isn't only going back to our old life, it can be standing still while God is moving on.

The creative mind produces an idea; the average mind produces a verdict.

Some people say they are waiting on the Lord when the Lord is on up ahead saying, "Will you come on!" Some people would make Hamlet look impetuous.

Sometimes we mistake the calling and the being sent forth. Moses was *called* at 40 years of age, but *sent forth* at 80. If we leave before our time, we will have to maintain our ministry on our own strength. The forecast: burnout.

The average person drives 12,000 to 20,000 miles per year which translates into 500 to 1000 hours per year or three to six months of 40 hour weeks. This is equivalent to one or two University semesters. Invest in some "How To" cassette tapes and turn your car into a classroom on wheels.

Dress to the level you aspire to be. Appearance contributes to reality.

It is a sad thing to trade today for tomorrow. It is a much sadder thing to trade today for yesterday.

You are where you go, because where you go determines whom you meet; whom you meet determines how you think; how you think determines what you do; and what you do determines your destiny.

CHARACTER

The ten sins that cause us to lose our way in realizing our greatest potential: 1) anger 2) resentment 3) fear 4) worry 5) desire to dominate 6) selfishness 7) guilt 8) sexual immorality 9) jealousy 10) lack of love for others which turns our hearts to stone.

Knowledge does not build character; faithfulness builds character.

The highest reward for our labor is not what we *get* from it, but what we *become* from it.

To act and not react is the essence of control.

You cannot separate character from conduct; you will act out who you are.

An unreliable man is brother to the saboteur.

The saddest person with the worst case of myopia is the person who cons himself.

"We come into the world with clenched fists; we go out with open hands." (*Hebrew Proverb*)

"Many people believe they're thinking when, in fact, they're only rearranging their prejudices."

(*Edward R. Murrow*)

If you watch too many soap operas you will begin to have soap opera problems.

Maturity: Putting off immediate gratification for the sake of long-term gains.

The way of the world is to take the line of least resistance—the easy way; but in the end we face great difficulty. God's way is difficult at first but gets easier as faith and trust grow.

I don't know of one man who, without God's help, can tame the monkeys that gibber in our loins.

The mind is like a house. Who would open the front door to let a fierce dragon in? It is easier to bar the door and keep him out than to wrestle him and expel him once he's inside. Be careful about what you allow to enter your mind.

When will I stop asking myself, "What will others think?" and begin asking, "What is the right thing to do?"

God calls us to be faithful, not successful.

One definition of maturity: the lack of a need to bring attention to one's self.

God spent a few days getting the Hebrew people out of Egypt. He spent 40 years getting Egypt out of the people.

Sin will...
take us farther than
we want to go;
keep us longer than
we want to stay;
cost us more than
we want to pay.

One of the indications of character has to do with a person's resiliency. Can they bend in the midst of the storms of life? A high wind will push an oak tree over. It will snap off a pine tree six to ten feet up from its base.

The palm tree, on the other hand, can stand the strain of hurricane force winds. Because it bends and lets the storm pass over, it does not break. God wants us to be like the palm tree. Resiliency allows us to persevere.

The noble man
makes noble plans
and by noble deeds
he stands.

(Isaiah 32:8)

JOY

Carl Walenda, the great high wire aerialist, said: "Only on the wire is there life; everything else is merely waiting." If you feel this way about your work, you will never work another day in your life because your work will have become your play. You'll be jealous of the sleep that robs you from your work. Vacations? They'll almost be an interruption.

The person having fun will always outperform the person who works out of a sense of duty.

The paradox about football: 70,000 people in the stands in need of exercise, watching 22 people on the field in need of rest.

Many in our frenetic, hard-charging, competitive, results-oriented society say, "Don't just stand there, do something!" God says, "Don't just do something—wait on Me and you will mount up with wings like eagles."

I hear people lament when approaching the big 3-0. And, upon reaching 40, they are almost distraught. I would rather be 60 years young than 30 years old. Each day is a gift and hopefully brings us closer to wisdom, to realizing the real purpose of life. It isn't *how long* we live that really matters, but *how* we live.

We've all heard the haunting question, "Did they die in vain?" The more significant question is, "Did they *live* in vain?"

Joy is different than happiness. Happiness is caused by outside influences. Joy is internal and springs not from a sense of who we are, but whose we are. We can have joy in the midst of turmoil.

If we do not forgive people for their transgressions, we ourselves become the victims of our own bitterness. The malignancy of our animosity cuts off our joy. I know people who are bitter with resentment over offenses when they have long forgotten the cause of them.

Joy is a cure for jealousy.

We seem to accept people until they violate some standard we have imposed upon them, whether or not we have expressed it. This becomes an irreparable breach between us, and they are forever *persona non grata* in our eyes. Life is much too short to let petty grievances fracture priceless relationships and rob us of the joy we can take in them.

TRUTH

One of the dumbest things I've ever heard a smart man say was said by Ted Turner. He said he believes that the Ten Commandments are passé. Once again, there's proof that smart and wise are not synonymous.

The voice of the minority is not often listened to, but truth cannot be resolved by numbers.

Today, we view tolerance as a virtue, more highly revered than truth.

Somewhere on our pilgrimage we must turn around and walk towards the Son, for light rejected leads to greater darkness.

Plato said, "Know thyself." The Greek mind held that truth came from within. The Hebraic mindset maintained that truth was outside of you, that is, a life source. This validates the importance of plugging into a God-believing, Bible teaching church.

In working toward the ideal, it is immature to ignore reality. Conversely, to live only with reality and fail to strive for the ideal only leads to cynicism and bitterness.

Better than searching for the meaning of life, search for God who gives meaning to life.

How does one defend a lion? One doesn't. All one has to do is open the cage door. The lion is perfectly capable of defending itself. And so it is with the first book ever published for wide distribution and consistently the number one best seller year after year since 1611. The Bible is not a history book that can be refuted, but a book on how to live life. One does not have to defend the Bible.

Abraham Lincoln said that if you don't lie you don't need a good memory. The truth is the truth is the truth.

Truth vs. expediency: Truth and honesty keep our moral feet to the fire. Expediency is self-serving and takes the line of least resistance.

The great curse of today is relativity. Modern man does not want to accept absolutes.

Faith

Obedience is both the test of and the evidence of faith.

Faith is rejecting our senses for the sake of hope.

Limited faith is controlled by circumstances and motivated by fear of failure.

There is no such thing as selective belief; Christianity is not a smorgasbord.

Seeing is not believing; believing is the beginning of seeing.

God has no grandchildren; you're either a child of God or you're not.

While the Declaration of Independence is revered in our republic, it is a declaration of dependence that matters in things eternal.

When Robert Fulton was working on his steamboat, most of the people standing on the shore observing his efforts day after day said he would never get it to float without capsizing. When it went steaming up the Hudson river in 1807, they said he would never get the thing to stop. Some people will never believe.

Instead of the prosaic greeting, "How are you doing?" or "How's everything going?" the next time you greet a brother or sister in the Lord, ask them, "How's your ministry?" Many of their responses will remind you of a tree full of owls hooting, "who...who." They haven't thought about a ministry in years.

It's only with the heart that one sees clearly the things which cannot be perceived by the eye.

Christianity is something like a slow-moving train. Some people board the train and ride awhile. Some people get on, get off, get on, get off, before they decide to stay either on or off. Some get on and almost immediately realize that it is the freedom train.

The skeptic says revelation, then belief. God says, first belief, then revelation.

There are more people in need of a faith life than are in need of a face lift.

We live in radical times. Radical times call for radical Christianity. Today, radical Christianity is merely uncompromising Christianity.

St. Francis of Assisi said, "Preach Jesus, and if necessary, use words." Our walk talks and our talk walks, but our walk talks louder than our talk walks.

John Grogan is available to speak on a wide variety of topics including:

- How to Get Things Done Thru Self Management
- How to Turn Individuals Into Results-Oriented Teams
- How to Turn One Time Buyers Into Lifetime Clients
- How to Work With All Kinds of People
- Managing Multiple Assignments
- The Seven Keys to Greatness *and much more!*

Here are what some people have said about him:

"You do a superb job of communication, teaching and motivating." —*Dr. Norman Vincent Peale*

"You are the Bob Hope of the American sales force. Every person in America needs to hear your message."

—*Jim Dale, Professional Trainer*
Member of the National Speakers Association

"The only speaker I would ever recommend, and I've been in a position to hear many."

—*Renee Jackson, State of Tennessee,*
Human Resources Office

"John, we've heard many comments like, 'He's believable,' and 'This guy gave me something I can use right now.'" —*Lumber Association of So. California*

For more information, please call: 1-800-230-1218
Or write: John Grogan Seminars International,
49 Chandler Rd., Mt. Juliet, TN 37122.